CONTENTS

D1711652

ABOUT *FIND THAT JOB!*

Can you really learn enough in just one hour to help you to find the right job? The answer is a resounding "Yes". This book provides you with a blueprint which will point you in all of the right directions, and gives you lots of tips and techniques that will take the luck out of the job hunting process.

The 60 Minutes Success Skills Series is written for people with neither the time nor the patience to trawl through acres of jargon, management-speak and page-filling waffle. Like all the books in the series, *Find That Job!* has been written in the belief that you can learn all you really need to know quickly and without hassle. The aim is to distil the essential, practical advice you can use straight away.

How to use this book

The message here is "It's OK to skim". Feel free to flick through to find the help you most need. This book is a collection of hands-on tips which will help you to spot any shortcomings you might have and show you how to turn them into strengths.

Divided into five chapters, *Find That Job!* deals with all the key issues that face everyone when looking for a job. Take 60 minutes to find out how to make yourself irresistible to potential employers. The book has been written to provide help both for older, more experienced job seekers as well as people just trying to start off in the work place.

As you read through the book, you will come across lots of tips and practical advice on how to make a big impact when seeking work. You could start by just going straight to any of the boxed features, which will ask you either to think about a problem or to do something about it and give you some ideas. If you're really pushed for time, you can always go direct to the tips features at the end of each chapter.

GOOD LUCK

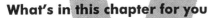

What's in this chapter for you

Targeting the right job
Planning the job hunt
The "All about me and what I've done" file
Face it – nobody's perfect!
Plugging the gaps
Suiting yourself
Networking

> ❝ *It seems to me that I take one step forward and two back.*
> *I know I should be higher up the career ladder than I am, and I keep*
> *sending off application forms, but I never get anywhere. Where I*
> *work presently, I can't seem to make any headway either. Others*
> *around me with a lot less ability than me seem to get the promotions.*
> *I am now just going through the motions and beginning to*
> *believe that I am never going to get lucky* ❞
> **– James Millar, accounts clerk**

Does James' experience sound at all familiar? Do you know you could be doing better and fulfilling your potential but feel that you are continually being thwarted in your efforts to find the perfect job?

Many ambitious people work hard at improving their lot in life. They send endless letters and applications, phone up recruitment companies continuously in the hope that they are ultimately going to "get lucky".

In most cases, luck has very little to do with finding the right job. Arnold Palmer, one of golf's greats, summed it up perfectly. He reckoned that the more he practised, the luckier he got! Job hunting is a mixture of:

a) Hard work,
b) Planning,
c) Creativity and
d) A little luck.

However, without a), b) and c), then in 99 per cent of cases d) will not apply.

Planning the job hunt

Your starting point when job hunting has got to be with yourself. You need to prepare for the task ahead in a very single-minded way and accept that, like anything that needs to be done properly, it will take you time.

> At the outset you must do a "personal audit" of your skills and abilities. By doing so, you can start to target the sorts of jobs that you are interested in and the sorts of employers who will be interested in you.

" Somehow I got it into my head when I left college with my degree that I could walk into a job as a computer programmer – I'd heard how good the money was! Even though I did not have a computer background, I kept applying for jobs and kept getting rejected. In the end, I went to a careers office and they advised me to either do a one-year computer studies course, then start applying, or forget it altogether. I did the course successfully and today I have a team of 15 programmers reporting to me! "
– Claire Essen, computer analyst

Claire's experience is really worth learning from. When looking for the perfect job, you need to make sure that you have the basic skills and qualifications in the first place. If you don't, then you will have to be amazingly resilient to take all of the rejection!

> Answer the following questions:
>
> ☐ *What would your dream job be?*
> ☐ *Do you need special qualifications? If so, can you realistically get these qualifications? Are you prepared to work really hard to get the right job?*
> ☐ *What do you consider your strengths to be over your competitors? How can you emphasise these to your potential employer?*

❑ *Are you being clinical enough about your search? Are you keeping the right records, following up on deadlines and generally being highly organised?*

Let's start by looking at what records you need to keep.

The "All about me, and what I've done" file

This particular weapon is absolutely vital and you should spend time in ensuring it is as full as possible. Refer to it whenever you are in the act of job hunting, even if you are simply making an informal enquiry.

When compiling the essential "about me" dossier, be absolutely truthful about yourself. Think honestly about your strengths and weaknesses – for absolute veracity check what you've written with a friend or a loved one, someone whose opinion you trust and who will be frank with you.

This file should include all of the following:

○ Comprehensive **personal** details, including full name, date of birth, address and telephone number. Other details such as place of birth, marital status, children etc. should be recorded here too, but you need to decide for yourself whether this kind of information is relevant when filling in application forms in the future. In some countries, questions about race, age or marital status are rightly illegal.
○ Your **educational** background. Record here the schools you attended from the age of 11 upwards and all of your academic qualifications. Again much of this is not going to be of use but keep it to hand just in case.
○ Your **further training**. This could prove especially important and should not include solely the achievements which give recognised qualifications. For example, by noting any computer related skills – even if you can only think of a three-hour session when a spreadsheet package was explained – it could help in persuading a future employer of your computer literacy.

○ **Other skills** and **hobbies**. This section might include details of hobbies or specific talents – such as fluency in a language or in amateur dramatics – which may help tip the balance in your favour. You should also list here membership of any relevant organisations (such as the Chamber of Commerce or a professional institute) which may help to show your commitment to a given industry.

○ **Employment history**. List the most recent jobs you have done first and go back as far as any holiday jobs you may have had to do when undertaking further education.

So, what's the point of recording that you passed your cycling proficiency test when you were twelve and that you like to spend the long winter evenings making quilts for voles? Well, it's just possible that your potential employer organises regular sponsored bicycle rides in support of rodent charities . . .

Obviously, much of what you have recorded in your "About me" file will never go into the public domain. However, it is essential that you have as much information about yourself as is possible, just in case. You will find it much easier to fill out application forms if you have a full dossier to hand and it will also help to reinforce your strengths in an interview situation when otherwise you might have dried up.

❝ It was my wife who organised a dossier on me and at the time I didn't think it was worth while – too much information going back too far. But at the second interview, when there was some probing of the obvious gaps in my direct experience, I managed to use the fact that I was a corporal in the sea scouts for six years to persuade them that I did have leadership skills. I am sure that having researched myself so thoroughly meant I had answers to tough questions at my fingertips. ❞
– Charles Fox, senior surveyor

Think of job hunting as a selling exercise. What you are doing by thinking of and collating information is to gain product knowledge. Don't forget – that product is YOU!

Again, get someone who knows you well and who will be honest with you to impartially look at the information you have recorded here. Accept suggestions and insights that they may have into your personality.

So you have started the job quest by noting your achievements up until this date. The next step is to try to analyse yourself as a person and how your strengths and weaknesses might affect your chances of landing the perfect job.

Horses for courses!

Although a potential employer is going to be judging you first of all from your letter of application and your CV, you need to be able to assess yourself (and therefore your chances of success for a given position) against a wide range of criteria.

Think carefully about the following factors and their relevance to your job hunting:

○ *Your Age:* In these anti-ageist times, it is not politically correct to consider age as a barrier to any job – indeed in many countries it would be illegal to do so. However, be realistic: some environments and companies will lend themselves to younger people and you should try to accept this and not waste too much energy in trying to get a result from such places.

Does the company you are considering applying to operate an (albeit unofficial) "youth only" policy, by appointing younger, and therefore cheaper, staff? Could your age preclude you from even getting an interview? Does the advertisement have any clues? Does it use words such as "young and dynamic" or "full training given?" If so, you might have to accept that they may be looking for someone else.

○ *Health:* Do you suffer from any conditions that would preclude you from doing certain types of work? For example, if you suffer from bad asthma then a job involving lifting or climbing may well cause you problems.

> Will you be able to cope physically and mentally with the types of job you are after?

○ **Personal Appearance:** Now, obviously, many aspects of your appearance will come down to personal opinions of the people you meet, but you need to ask yourself the following questions:
  – Are you as neat and tidy as the company needs you to be?
  – Is there anything about your physical appearance that could be off-putting in a first encounter, such as excessive body-piercing, tattoos etc?
  – Is your personal hygiene up to scratch? If you smoke, do your clothes and hair stink of tobacco? If so, what can you do about it, as this sort of thing can really put a potential employer off?

❝ On paper, Sarah's application looked perfect. However, when she turned up for the interview, it was obvious she'd had quiet a few cigarettes in the last hour to steady her nerves. I'm afraid I didn't offer her the job in the surgery because of it, which was a shame as in every other respect she was an excellent applicant ❞
– Rose Cooper, dentist

Other questions you may need to ask yourself (and be honest!) are:

○ How sharp witted are you? Are you sure that you have what it takes to handle the job you are after? Are you versatile enough to learn new skills and will you be responsive to training?
○ If you don't have the right qualifications to do the job, can you convince yourself, and a potential employer, that your experience alone will be enough to get you by?
○ Do you have all the necessary skills you will need for this position? For example, are your verbal communication skills up to scratch? Can you write well enough? If you have doubts about your skill levels, can you do anything about them by way of training courses or self-teaching?
○ Are you good with people? If a job is looking for a team player and you consider yourself to be something of a loner, then are you likely to succeed? Are you a leader or a follower?
○ Do you have a good sense of humour?

The above is by no means an exhaustive list of your character traits – the point of it all is to be able to make a fair assessment of the sort of person you are, so that you can fit yourself into the job. Don't worry if you are quiet and shy – not every job requires a raving extrovert. However, if the job you are after involves entertaining hundreds of people, then it may well be the wrong job for you!

> ❝ *I was forced into a career change in my late 30s after I was made redundant. I didn't want to stay in manufacturing, but didn't know what else I could do. I went to a counsellor who did an audit of my skills and experience and she helped me to realise that my talents lent themselves exactly to the training environment. I love it!* ❞
> **– Chris Wiley, management trainer**

Plugging the gaps

If you have been honest with yourself, you should have realised what weaknesses you may have in terms of the new job you are looking for. So what can you do about them?

> If your self-assessment reveals lots of problems, gaps and inadequacies then don't despair! Nobody is perfect. Everyone sees flaws in themselves and you may well just be being over-critical. But whatever your genuine shortcomings may be, you can do something about them!

Here are some typical problem areas and some hot tips for overcoming them.

Health

If your physical activity extends only as far as opening the fridge door to take out another can of beer, and even this leaves you a sweating wreck hardly able to pick your cigarette up, then you probably have two problems. The first is that you are unlikely to live long enough to finish reading this book, the second is that if you are seriously unfit and unhealthy, then this will cause you problems both at the interview stage and when you find work.

Give up all of your vices, train for months on end, and eat like an athlete until you have developed an Olympian physique. No, seriously, doing a little light exercise will make you feel better about yourself, and will improve your chances at an interview (unless of course your interviewer is a chain-smoking, obese, alcoholic, glue sniffer in which case this advice is irrelevant). It should also make you feel much more energetic.

Qualifications

If your lack of formal qualifications is proving a major drawback in your quest for the perfect job, then commit to extra relevant study. This will look good on an application, and may persuade someone to take you on even if you're only part-qualified (and they may even pay the rest of the course fees!).

However, as we said earlier, be realistic. If you have spent all your life as an account clerk in the city, it is unlikely that night-school physics will qualify you for that key post at NASA.

To plug the gaps in your qualifications:

☐ *Set your sights on realistic qualifications*
☐ *Talk to others who are doing courses in their spare time and find out about costs and the possible difficulties involved in part-time study*
☐ *Investigate what help you could receive to go back to full-time studying.*

Skills

If your communication skills, either verbal or written, appear to be a problem, then you can take action. You can go on courses to improve your writing skills, and there are some excellent books and software packages around which will help you to write well. Similarly, if you lack confidence when speaking in front of an audience, then try a public speaking course or the various tapes and books which are on the market. If you can't find any, or can't afford them, then practise in front of friends or relatives.

In this technological day and age, handwriting skills are less and less important. However, most potential employers will ask for a hand-written letter in support of applications, so you need to do something if your handwriting is barely legible or very unattractive. Take time to practise. If necessary, talk to junior schoolteachers if you know any. Work on it!

> Recognise your weaknesses and address them! Commit to positive action to overcome them.

Suiting yourself

Regardless of your situation – whether you have been unemployed for some time, or are facing redundancy at what you consider to be a "difficult" age, or are just starting off your career – you need to draw up a list of requirements that a potential job must have for you. Unless you are absolutely desperate (and probably destitute as well) our message is that job hunting is a two-way thing. You have got to be comfortable and happy with the company that you are considering joining. The Victorian work ethic ("You're damn lucky to have a job anywhere") should be a thing of the past.

> 66 *I'd taken time out from a successful career to bring up my two children and was looking for a way back in. However, I hadn't decided whether I wanted full-time or part-time work. Eventually the perfect full-time job came up but I hesitated because it meant I had to commute and the hours were long. Consequently the offer was withdrawn and I was back to square one. If only I'd had it clear in my mind what it was I was after, I could maybe have secured a reduced hours position.* 99
> **– Dawn Miller, solicitor**

When considering what job you are looking for, think of the following and how important they may be to you:

○ **Location:** Are you prepared to travel long distances to get to work? Have you considered the strain this may put on you and your loved ones? Have you considered the cost?

○ **Status:** Is a grand-sounding job title important to you?
○ **Salary:** Are you prepared to compromise on what you consider yourself to be worth in the market place? Is salary more important than job satisfaction or the chance to break into an exciting career environment, albeit at a low level?
○ **Travel:** Being away from home a lot, especially overseas, may sound glamorous and exciting, but you need to consider carefully whether this kind of life will suit you. Can you cope with being on your own, missing out perhaps on your social life at home? What sort of strains will it put on you and your family?
○ **Prospects:** How important is job security to you? Are you prepared to take a job which is risky but challenging, or are you after the safer option of security. Are you prepared to move into a new field (perhaps management for the first time) with the associated risks this may hold?
○ **Pressure:** Are you ready to take on a job which is highly pressured? Can you and those around you cope?
○ **The future:** Is the job you are looking for something which you see as merely a stepping-stone to bigger and better things, or do you see it as a long-term commitment?

Never forget just how much of your life is absorbed by work. You owe it to yourself to make sure you get the *right* job.

Networking

The idea of networking has slightly unpleasant, sycophantic undertones to certain people. However, there is nothing wrong with mixing in the right circles and getting your face known. You can do this by joining the right organisations and groups – such as professional bodies, local chambers of commerce and such like – and attending conferences and exhibitions. The cost may be prohibitive if you are currently unemployed, but there may well be opportunities to meet people which won't cost much and will be useful.

A major advantage of being well networked is that you might find jobs coming to you via word of mouth, which gives you an edge from the start.

To get the right job you need to look carefully and honestly at yourself and the jobs you apply for.

1. Finding the right job is a full-time job in itself. Commit your time and effort properly, and you will be rewarded!
2. Competition for certain jobs is intense and you will not succeed every time. When you are unsuccessful, learn lessons from the experience – what can you do better next time?
3. Take an impartial view of what you can offer by way of previous experiences. Start a dossier on yourself which lists your achievements and experience. Make it as detailed as possible – you never know when a small piece of information remembered in an interview could prove vital!
4. Commit to plugging gaps. If you have weaknesses and they can be overcome by extra study or reading appropriate books, then do it! The more you put in, the greater will be the rewards.
5. Ask yourself if your ambitions are realistic. Are you physically and mentally healthy enough? Do you truly have the right personality?

This chapter should have helped to clarify in your own mind what it is you are offering to a future employer and what positions you should target. You are now ready to proceed to actively finding that job!

What's in this chapter for you

Planning your CV/résumé
Make it fit
What to include
Writing strong covering letters
Speculative applications
Filling application forms

❝ *I was very naive after I left college. I really thought my first CV was a masterpiece – eight pages of autobiographical nuggets! It wasn't until a friend of mine in a recruitment agency put me straight that I started getting interviews.* ❞
– Graham Hopkins, sales manager

You should by now have done the background work, and thought through the issues with regard both to what kind of job you want, and what kind of job you are likely to get. It is now time to think how you get the right information into the hands of potential employers.

The curriculum vitae/résumé

Let's define our terms from the start – we are a going to use the term CV throughout this book for the very good reason that it is a lot shorter to type than *personal history* and, unlike *résumé*, it doesn't contain accents. We apologise if it is not the term you use in your country but your annoyance should be diminished in the knowledge that you are getting more words of wisdom per page as a result of it.

Your CV is probably the single most important tool in your job hunting armoury. It is the main thing that you must get right in order to get you noticed and achieve your primary goal – an interview!

Most books about finding a job will give you pages of samples of what the ideal CV should look like. We are different. We will stick simply to giving you advice as to what the content should be.

> There is one golden rule: Your CV is not carved in granite (unless, possibly, you are after a job as a stonemason). Every job you go after will be different, and you need to slant your CV accordingly. If you send the same CV all of the time, then you will be greatly reducing your chances of success.

When planning your CV, look for the hidden messages that job adverts contain and skew the experience you have had accordingly. For example:

○ *"Must be able to work in a busy environment" probably means the job is highly pressured, with phones ringing all of the time etc. – bring out forcefully how you have risen to relevant challenges in the past (even if you've only worked in a busy pub as a college job).*
○ *"Self-starter needing constant challenges" is a phrase often used by companies that don't believe in structured management. Thus, stress your self-motivation and your desire for a position with a degree of autonomy.*

Get the picture? Try to read between the lines and give a potential employee what they want! Let's now look at some of the most commonly asked questions about CVs.

"How long is the perfect CV?"

The simple answer here is: "it all depends on your circumstances". If you are straight out of school then you frankly don't have a lot to say except for details of qualifications and other personal information deemed relevant – you should provide no more than two pages and back it up with personal references.

If however, you are in the early stages of a career after further education, then you could possibly stretch this to two to three pages, as you will have more information to get across. In general, a CV should not go beyond three pages in our view, even if you have thirty years' relevant experience to get across. People will just get bored reading it.

> Resist the temptation to pad out your CV. If you can't think of anything further of relevance to include then stop.

"What sort of paper and design should I use?"

Our advice is to keep it simple. A CV will look smart and professional if produced using a standard typeface on a good quality white paper. In our experience, providing photographs of yourself is not a good idea. If you resemble the rear end of a farm animal then you are going to put people off. If you look like a movie star you may well get interviewed for the wrong reasons. More likely your application will be turned down on the grounds of gross arrogance!

Have you heard people recommend the use of coloured paper so that the application "stands out"? There may be some merit in this but there is also a downside – CVs will often be copied for circulation in a company and the chances are that your coloured paper will not copy clearly. You will then be giving the impression of having provided a poor quality CV.

"Should I use an agency to produce my CV professionally?"

In most cases, the answer here is "no". If you are just starting out in your career, the chances are that the cost would be too prohibitive anyway. Access to a PC and a reasonable printer will provide you with a perfectly adequate finished article.

Other CV tips

- ❑ *Avoid technical language unless you are sure it is absolutely necessary – you may come across as a techno-nerd.*
- ❑ *Do not always assume that the first person to look at your CV will be the person who will be making the decision about the appointment. Very often in larger companies, a secretary or some other support staff will make the initial selection to be passed on to the boss – if your CV is too jargon ridden, then you may well not make it into the "possibles" file.*
- ❑ *Tailor your CV to each application you make by cutting detail you know will not be of interest and reinforcing parts which you know will be your best selling points.*
- ❑ *Learn from experience – if your CV doesn't appear to be having the desired result (i.e. getting you an interview) change it!*

> ❝ *I always remember the first time I had to recruit a junior copy writer. I was presented with a pile of over 150 CVs to go through. On the first scan, most were virtually identical. I then came across one that was just one side of A4 paper with the barest details included. At the bottom it said "Want to know more? Ask me for an interview". I was really struck by the audacity and was convinced right then that he was the person for the job. As it turned out, he was a complete idiot and lasted only 15 minutes at the interview but the point was his CV got him noticed.* ❞
> **– Chris Rally, advertising executive**

In certain work environments, a "cheeky" CV such as described by Chris above might just work. However it is a risky strategy and should only really be tried experimentally and only when trying to get a position in a "creative" environment.

What to put on the CV

The basics you can take as read – full name, address, telephone number etc. As discussed before, some more sensitive data, such as marital status, number of children and even date of birth, can be left off in certain circumstances. If you have a full clean driving licence and this is relevant, then include this information.

You should then include details of where you were educated from the age of 11 onwards. (If you are a recent graduate you can include here any positions or offices you held at college if and only if they give an impression of hard work and sobriety!)

> ❝ *You'd be amazed at how many people think it relevant to include the fact that they were milk monitors at primary school! When you read unnecessary detail like that it either means the applicant has nothing else to say about themselves or they are completely out of touch with the real world!* ❞
> **– Kathy Dedington, personnel director**

Next you should outline your qualifications in chronological order starting with your achievements at school. You don't need to include grades attained for anything other than higher education – and don't be tempted to lie about your school achievements!

You might just get asked to prove the existence of that basket-weaving qualification!

You should give details of any further training that you have undertaken if you deem it relevant. This will help to give the impression that you are keen to improve yourself and learn skills that will help you in your professional life.

" My pop art degree was really done out of a spirit of self-indulgence. I wanted a job in business but was having great difficulty in getting anyone to take me seriously. Eventually I went on a short course to teach me basic business and office skills. I added this information to my CV and subsequently I had a lot more success in obtaining interviews – it showed my versatility. "
– Greg Rodgers, marketing manager

Your employment history is important, even if you are straight out of school and have only had casual jobs. By listing the jobs you did and stressing any responsibility you have had, you will be making yourself much more attractive to a potential employer.

For those readers who are further down the career path than this, list your most recent jobs first and give the approximate dates you served. You should normally give most detail about your more current experience.

" Some of the CVs we get here beggar belief. Men of 45 spend half a page telling us about their first crucial job in a boiler room in 1966. We want snappy information on a person's distant past and a lot of detail of what they have been doing in the last, say, five years "
– Kathy Dedington, personnel director

Give the brief details of who you worked for, with an emphasis on your job title and responsibilities. Now is your chance stress any major achievements that you feel are relevant. You may also wish to give briefly the reasons why you moved on. Stress the positive – "my boss was a cretin" might be a truthful reason for leaving a position, but "career enhancement" gives a somewhat more favourable slant to it!

" You can tell from what people write down as their achievements exactly what sort of person they are. We had one guy write "In the

10 years I was plant manager we only had three fatalities on site"!
Is that something to be proud of? How many fatalities
did he have off site?! **"**
– Kathy Dedington

> Accentuate the positive when reviewing your past career. If you
> were part of a successful team, don't try to accept all of the
> credit as that would be dishonest (and you may be found out if
> they take a reference from someone you worked with at that
> time) but stress the satisfaction gained by all. This will show
> what a great team player you can be.

Leisure interests are something which should definitely be included
when you are at the beginning of your career and you don't have
a lot to offer by way of work experience to show the kind of
person that you are.

Mention hobbies and sports and stress any activity which shows
you have some leadership qualities, such as captaining a team or
being chair of a society. You may wish to be selective about what
you tell a future employee if some of your extra-curricular
activities could in any way be deemed unusual or controversial.
This might include religious or political affiliations – should you
feel very strongly about anything of this nature then by all means
mention it at the interview stage.

" *I know it is wrong of me but if I ever see that someone is*
into morris dancing, they immediately get put to the bottom of the
pile! I'm not sure I'd have such a strong reaction if they included
arson as a hobby! I've just got this aversion to middle-class men
prancing around with bells on their shoes! **"**
– Kathy Dedington

Kathy's is obviously an extreme view of folk-dancing and not one
the author condones in any way. However, be aware that some
people may take (misguided) exception to certain activities – you
may wish to address this but wait until you have got your foot in
the door!

Some experts recommend that you should next list your
professional objectives and goals – a "why I want this job"

statement. It is up to you. The strategy can cause problems if you are obviously overqualified for a post: it will be pretty obvious that your ambitions will mean that you are only looking at the job as a stepping stone to something better. If you want to adopt this tactic, keep it short, sweet and realistic.

Finally, you should include the names of two referees. If you are new to the job market then use people who know you personally such as teachers or anyone local in a position of respect. If you are more experienced, then use present or past employers. You may wish to add a rider to this to say that you do not wish references to be taken up without prior consultation.

Select your referees carefully as you need to be sure that they can, when necessary, properly persuade a potential employee of your strengths. Brief the referee beforehand so that they understand fully the kind of work you are looking for and say why you think your talents lend themselves to this work.

❝ I remember phoning up for a reference for a recent school leaver from his former class teacher. He was waxing lyrical about the boy's talents but then let slip that he was rather shy in front of more than a couple people. The job we were going to offer him involved a lot of customer contact and despite the fact that he interviewed well, I'm afraid we didn't offer him the job. ❞
– Jill Peters, bank personnel officer

In any case, make sure that get the agreement of your potential referees well in advance. If your job hunting is taking a long time (say over 3 months) then it is polite and sensible to keep asking for their support.

Covering letter

Normally, your covering letter should be in your own handwriting. Most employers will want to see that you are indeed literate (and that you can spell without the aid of a spellchecker program!). Golden rules here are:

○ *Use a good-quality pen that won't run out half way through. Black ink is probably best as it will photocopy better.*

○ *Space the letter well so that it covers the whole page.*

○ *Write clearly and neatly, and keep a check on your spelling and grammar.*

○ *If you make a mistake, start again. Correction fluid or scoring out errors looks sloppy.*

○ *Refer clearly to both the job you are after and where you saw it advertised – the company may be on a recruitment drive and have advertised lots of different positions in different places all at once.*

○ *Convey briefly why you think the job should be yours. Refer this back to the information given in the job advertisement so that you hit them immediately with the obvious reasons for inviting you for interview.*

Again, keep it simple! Make sure that the person to whom you are writing's name, position and full company address are written in the top left of the page and your address is in the top right. Sign and print your name at the bottom and finish the letter properly: if you are writing to a named individual (i.e. "Dear Mr Jones") use "Yours sincerely". If it is to "Dear Sir/ Madam" finish the letter "Yours faithfully".

> **❝** *We employ about eight school leavers a year and, quite honestly, it makes me despair for the educational standards being set. We get application forms sent in that look like the dog has chewed it. Accompanying letters arrive with words crossed out, and spelling mistakes on every line. Rightly or wrongly, it just puts me off people, and even if they are top class academically, the sloppiness of their application means they don't even get an interview.* **❞**
> **– Thomas Miller, MD of a clothing manufacturer**

Accuracy, grammar, correct forms of address are old-fashioned concepts. However, they do still matter and most employers will value them. Make sure that everything you write is spelt correctly, that the grammar is accurate and that the text is well laid out and clear.

Remember to keep a copy of your letter so you can remind yourself of what you said before an interview.

The speculative letter

So far in this book, we have looked at how you should apply for an advertised job. However, depending on your circumstances, you may well be trying the "cold-call" approach. It may be that you are well known in your given industry, with a network of contacts who will respond to an approach from you, or at least take notice. However, if you are new to the job market or trying to get into a particular industry for the first time, your chances of success speculatively are slim.

Find out about the company and what it does (more on this later) but, more importantly, find out the names of the key people and use them. If the company is large, write the same letter to the head of the relevant department and the personnel director. That way you double your chances of being remembered.

“ Like many companies, we have a policy of replying to unsolicited approaches with the standard "We'll keep you on file until a suitable position arises..." reply. This means nothing – the letters and CVs are filed for six months then chucked away. In all honesty, if a vacancy does arise then we tend to start from scratch with a new advertisement. A speculative approach has to be something pretty special to get a result. ”
– Gill Niven, legal partner

The key with the unsolicited approach is to make sure your letter is read and remembered. So, the golden rules of accuracy and neatness still apply, but you have to make an in impact quickly.

Let's imagine you are wanting to break into book publishing by becoming a sales representative. There is a local company nearby that you want to approach, but they have not advertised suitable positions for some time. Your speculative letter might read something like the one shown overleaf.

Your Full
Address

Mr D Tomes
Sales and Marketing Director
Good Publishing Ltd
33 Book Side
Remainder Lane
Summers Field
Kent

Tuesday, March 17, 1998

Dear Mr Tomes,
I am very interested in gaining employment in book publishing and
have long admired your organisation as a consumer. You will be
pleased to hear that, during my time in higher education, I used
many of the books that your company has published.

As a recent graduate, I have no practical experience to offer your
company. However, I am quick to learn, self-confident and highly
motivated. I work hard, am a good team player and love challenges.

I enclose my CV for your information. You will see from this that
apart from obtaining my degree in economics, I involved myself in
many other activities which have taught me good interpersonal skills.
I will telephone your office on the 19 March to discuss with you any
vacancies.

Yours sincerely

Your name

Cc Mr R Murdoch, Head of Personnel

The key to making speculative applications is boldness. Make
your letter interesting and confident, but most important of all,
follow up on the telephone.

> " *I was desperate to get into advertising but the right jobs never seemed to appear. I sent off loads of speculative letters, and steeled myself to make the follow up calls. In most cases I was told to stop pestering them, but I got on well in three companies. I got their agreement that I could phone in every month to see if there were any openings. Eventually, I was told of a forthcoming job, which was to be advertised. I applied in the normal way and got the job. My boss admits that she took me on because she was aware of my keenness and persistence.* "
> **– Rod Grant, copywriter**

Application forms

Some organisations require you to fill out one of their own application forms for any position. This will normally be sent out to you with some kind of job description.

Most application forms are fairly standard, asking you for all of the usual background information such as experience, qualifications etc. Where you have to do some work is in any section which asks you to describe any skills, achievements or experience which makes you particularly suitable for the position you are after.

The key with application forms is to study the job description (or people spec) closely, and make sure that you slant your comments to fit their criteria as closely as possible.

Try not to make your responses too obvious. If the job spec asks for "highly-organised, creative leadership", avoid trotting out "I am a highly organised creative leader because....". Rephrase what you want to say so that the obvious conclusion is going to be that you are the right person for the job.

Other tips for filling out application forms are:

❏ *Use a good-quality pen, with black ink, and make sure you keep it neat.*
❏ *Make a copy of the form and do a dummy run to make sure you space it all out properly. This is especially important if*

---

you have to fill out boxes with information on schooling or qualifications.

❑ *In the "Why do you think you are suitable?" box, most will say "Please continue on a separate sheet if you wish". Do so. You need enough space to make your case and to sell yourself. Use good-quality paper and don't be tempted to type.*

❑ *Once you've completed it, keep a copy!*

If you have mastered the art of putting together an arresting CV or filling out application forms in a persuasive way, the interview offers should start to flow.

Make your applications irresistible

1. Change your CV to fit the circumstances. Think of it as your flexible friend and adapt it to every different situation. Keep it up to date.
2. If you aren't getting asked for interviews, then change the structure of the CV and look carefully for weaknesses in your covering letters.
3. Don't be tempted to pad out your CV by putting in irrelevant or overly technical information.
4. Never lie on the CV or application form – you may well be found out and that will do your career prospects no good at all.
5. Always take a copy of any application letters or forms you send off – you don't want to inadvertently contradict yourself in an interview.
6. If you make "cold calls" when looking for work, be prepared to follow up on the telephone or you may well be wasting your time.

What's in this chapter for you

Bad timing
Feeling and looking good
First impressions count
Practice makes perfect
You and the position
Predicting the questions

❝ *After more than twenty applications, I finally got an interview. It was such a thrill, but I started to panic – what do I have to do now?!* ❞
– Shahzia Choong, desk editor

So, you've sent your beautifully prepared CV off and the longed-for letter inviting you to an interview duly drops on you mat. What now? First of all, congratulate yourself! Well done! You've already got further than most of the other applicants and you can afford to bask in glory for a few seconds. Now you have to get down to the important task of preparation.

Let's look at the letter you have received. It is going to tell you the basic details about when and where, and who you will see. It should also tell you if you will be required to make a presentation or to take a test of some sort.

Bad timing

What happens if the date and time given are inconvenient? Let's be honest, there's inconvenient and inconvenient. The golden rule here is that you should only try to reschedule an interview if you *absolutely* have to. Such circumstances might include a funeral of a close family friend, an examination or a hospital appointment, which cannot be moved. If any of these arise then you may have to kiss goodbye to the opportunity – very often interviews are only held on specific days and the interviewers will have busy schedules to meet. Consequently, it is unlikely that an interview will be rescheduled.

❝ I'd spent a long time filling out the application forms and was delighted to get an interview. Only trouble was it was on the same day as a really important away game in the cup for the local football team – I couldn't have made both. There was no way I could let the lads down so I phoned to reschedule. The personnel woman was really unreasonable and said something about me looking at my priorities. She wouldn't reschedule the interview so the whole thing was a waste of time. ❞
– Gary Trimble, amateur footballer

Poor Gary! What an unreasonable response from a large faceless organisation!

What if you have two interviews which clash? In this slightly unlikely event then you have to decide which job is the most suitable for you and commit to keeping that appointment. You should then get on the phone to your second choice immediately and ask to speak to the person who has written the letter and try to agree an alternative time. You have a choice here: either be honest or lie through your teeth.

❝ It was absolutely typical! I had not even had so much as a hint of an interview for about six months, then I got the offer of two on the same day at 10.00 and 11.00 in the morning 50 miles away from each other! I thought about inventing the sudden death and subsequent funeral of an aged but terribly close relative and trying to stall the company which I was slightly less interested in. But lying is not my style. I got on the phone, explained the predicament and they slotted me in last thing. To cap it all, that was the job I got offered and they are a great company to work for! ❞
Sandra James, secretary

If an interview is genuinely inconvenient, it is best to be honest with a company and try to change the appointment. If it proves impossible then so be it. Lying is unlikely to have made any difference at all but might eventually trip you up!

❝ I was asked to attend an interview 200 miles away! I couldn't afford to go unless the company helped with the travelling costs. However, this was not made clear on the letter. I was loath to phone them as I thought it might be a bit cheeky, so I borrowed the money. Throughout the interview, I was nervous and worried about how to

approach them about paying my expenses. I'm sure that's why I didn't get the job. **"**
– Dean Rabin, engineering graduate

If you are at all concerned as to whether the company will pay for you to attend an interview, the best policy is to phone them up and ask. As a general rule, if you are new to the job market then they should pay for you to attend. If you are more experienced and are currently in work then it is safe to assume that you will have to pay unless the interview means an exceptionally long journey to the other end of the country, perhaps by plane, and entails an overnight stop.

Work on the assumption that a company should make it clear in their invitation letter whether they are going to pay your expenses. If they don't, then phone them and ask. If they won't pay, ask yourself: a) Can you afford to attend? b) Is the risk that you might lose your money worth it? and c) Do you want to work for a tight-fisted company like this anyway?

Here are some tips for what else to do when you've heard you've got an interview:

○ *Confirm that you can attend, briefly and neatly in writing (if time permits), and make sure you are doing so to the right contact person.*
○ *If you have not been told, find out who you will be seeing – if you turn up expecting a one-on-one interview and are confronted by six besuited executives, you may be a tad daunted!*
○ *Plan your journey: whether it is near or far, allow yourself plenty of time so that you don't arrive sweating, dishevelled and late!*
○ *Plan what you are going to take with you and pack your case the night before. You will need a copy of your CV and application, paper for taking notes, questions you may have thought of in advance, a pen, possibly a calculator and, perhaps, samples of your work.*

Feeling and looking good

It is a simple fact of life that, no matter what a brilliant mind and sparkling personality God may have granted you, if you attend an interview looking like you have been dragged through a hedge backwards and then smeared with dung, you are unlikely to make the right impression. You have to plan on looking right.

Think about the following:

○ Hair: is bright green suitable for a job in a bank? Less extreme, perhaps, is your hair well groomed, clean and tidy. Would a hair cut be sensible? If you must have facial hair, trim it (this applies to men as well). Buy a new razor and get a good shave.
○ Personal hygiene: interviews are nerve wracking so use a strong deodorant. You don't want the interview to be curtailed after ten minutes for a fresh air break. And think about your breath – use a mouth freshener.
○ Keep things such as jewellery, perfumes or aftershave as well as loud clothes to an absolute minimum. OK, so you might feel that this is denying you the right to express yourself as an individual, but you don't know the values or mindsets of the people you will be meeting so our advice is to **play safe**.
○ Make sure that your clothes are clean and well ironed. Don't skimp on dry cleaning if it's necessary.

Mental preparation

Physically you should be looking good. You've now got to sort out your mental approach.

> **"** I seem to be able to talk myself out of jobs before I've even got through the front door! I go in thinking they won't want me – and so far they haven't **"**
> **– Jean Davis, administrator**

You need to work on your mental attitude now. No matter how many setbacks you might have had in the past – failed interviews, redundancy etc. etc. – you have to go into the interview believing that you can succeed.

As soon as you know your interview date, remind yourself of the following:

❑ You're successful already – you are one of the chosen few to have got this far!
❑ Your successes in career and in life so far.
❑ Say: "I can and will get this job – I know I am the right person for it."

First impressions

The impending interview situation is nothing short of a theatrical event. You play a part when you enter the room and the people interviewing are doing likewise (unless it's their hobby to fire questions at complete strangers).

> **"** *As soon as the door opens and a candidate enters, you get an immediate impression of what sort of person they are. If someone shuffles in, avoids eye contact, has a wet fish for a handshake, I'm afraid the interview is virtually over before it has even begun. Conversely, when you meet someone confident and assured, you really sit up and take notice.* **"**
> **– Wendy Talbot, marketing director**

First impressions do matter. So, start practising the following:

○ *On entering a room, stand tall, smile and walk confidently to greet your hosts.*
○ *Work on a firm, but not vice-like, handshake that can be altered in intensity to match the other person's. Don't try to break the other person's hand, but don't be dominated by a crushing grip from someone else.*
○ *Sitting with attitude. Sit upright with your arms in your lap or resting beside you. Sit in a relaxed manner with your feet together so that you cannot swing your legs, scratch a leg with a foot or display any other nervous traits.*

And, especially for the men, think about the length of your trousers when sitting down and the design of your socks. Is a senior executive really going to be impressed with your Winnie the Pooh socks?

Think also about how you speak. Do you tend to mumble, slur your words or speak at breakneck speed when you're nervous? If so, try taking deep breaths, keep your hands away from your face and concentrate on speaking slowly and clearly.

Don't worry if you have a strong regional accent – this should not make a difference to your chances in this day and age. Do worry if you have a tendency to over-use slang or colloquialisms – analyse your speech and try to correct any obvious faults.

Ask those around you who you respect and trust for their honest and impartial opinion of how you come over to strangers. Most people have certain nervous traits and habits. The best you can do is to try to minimise yours. And, don't get too hung up about them or else you'll never leave the house!

Practice makes perfect

Well, actually, it doesn't in the interview context! You can never predict precisely what is going to happen when you enter the interview room, but you can do some basic exercises to maximise your chances of making a good impression.

Video training

There are many courses available at which you can experience a mock interview. Often these are cheap to undertake and in some cases are free! It can be a horrifying experience when you actually see and, more importantly, hear yourself in a stressful situation. But remember, the technology distorts everything and you don't really look and sound quite so awful!

If it does not prove possible to experience a full-blown practice video session, then you can ask friends or family to give you a trial run. There was a reason for buying that camcorder, after all! However, this is only really useful in order for you to rehearse your answers to the predicted questions as opposed to honing your interview techniques. The situation is totally false and you will undoubtedly be embarrassed in front of someone close to you.

If you are worried about your speech, then use a tape recorder to listen to yourself and practise ironing out the problems. However, remember that this can be a shattering experience, as the voice will be horribly distorted!

What's it all about?

Now that you're physically and emotionally ready for the interview, you need to concentrate on acquiring the knowledge that you need about the company that you are hoping to join.

❝ *It's incredible how few interviewees actually seem to bother finding out the basics about our business. They know the name, but they haven't got a clue about our range of services or our success in the export markets. They seem to expect me to tell them everything. If they haven't the interest or the commitment to find out a bit about us beforehand, then how do they know they want to work for us?* **❞**
– David Connell, MD telecom industry

You need to do some basic research on the company before attending an interview (and in certain cases before even sending off your application – more on that later). You need to do this to show that:

○ *you really want a career with this company*
○ *you have initiative*
○ *you will suit the company*
○ *you are better than the other candidates.*

If you ensure you know in your own mind why you are there, you will find it far easier to persuade the interviewers of the same.

Bigger companies might well send you a starter pack of information about themselves. Obviously you should start by studying this and absorbing as much as is possible. However, we must assume that every candidate will do this, so how do you give yourself a greater competitive advantage? Here are some tips for finding out more.

You can find out more information on larger businesses by:

❑ *Looking in the various business directories in the library.*
❑ *Searching the Internet – a particularly good source for any press stories that may have appeared over the past few months.*
❑ *Annual reports – if you've not been sent one, ask!*

> ❏ *Personal contacts – perhaps you know of someone in a related business who knows the company you're seeing. What are their perceptions? How is the company perceived within the context of their industry?*
> ❏ *If the business is a limited company then previous financial records will be lodged at Companies House or your local equivalent. Normally for a small fee these records can be gained and will give you invaluable information on the financial strengths (or weaknesses!) of the company you are thinking of joining.*

You and the position

You should by this stage have received something along the lines of a job description. You've already got an interview so we assume that you are, on the whole, well suited to the position on offer but you may well have gaps in your experience. So, how do you plug these when you are asked about them (as you will be if the interviewer has any kind of professionalism)?

> Assess your training experience, similar roles you have experienced already or where your leisure experiences may count. If there are still gaps, think of the arguments to persuade them and yourself that they are not terribly important – you can pick them up as you go along.

It is unlikely that the perfect candidate, fitting exactly all of the criteria, exists for any job anywhere. So, there will always be some shortcomings with every candidate. If you are to be successful, concentrate on persuading the interviewers that you've got the right personality to succeed.

Shortfalls in experience can be made up for by hard work, enthusiasm and the willingness to obtain new skills through training – if you believe this yourself, you *will* convince your audience.

Predicting the questions

No two interviews are the same and you cannot hope to attend an interview having second-guessed all the questions that you are going to be asked (unless, perhaps, you are a clairvoyant). However, there are some questions which you can assume will probably be used. Here are some examples (although they may be phrased slightly differently):

What are your strengths/weaknesses?

In the view of this author, this is a lazy, unimaginative question. For strengths, you are unlikely to answer that you have a superhuman intellect and will be capable of running the business yourself within six weeks. Similarly, for weaknesses you are hardly likely to admit to a weak bladder and dipsomania. A bland question demands a bland answer. For strengths, think of your experience and achievements and how they imply a particular character trait (i.e. hardworking/quick thinking/strong leadership etc.). For weaknesses admit to a minor faux pas in the past that you are committed to rectify (e.g. "I've always been rather too impatient to get on in my career in the past. I think this position here will challenge me and keep me stimulated for the foreseeable future ...").

> Work on turning a possible weakness into a definite strength. Thus, admit to certain minor failings whilst at the same time demonstrating how you plan to overcome them. Never admit to a problem as being insurmountable.

How would you describe yourself?

This sometimes comes in the form: "How would a close member of your family describe you?" Here you need to think back to any character traits that the original job advertisement listed. So, if they wanted a cheerful extrovert who was great at Barry Manilow impressions, that is how you describe yourself (obviously rephrasing the original a little).

Why do you want to work here?

Stress the positive aspects of the company that you have learnt from your research. Avoid being overly flattering but support your answer with hard evidence. Thus, a reply such as "I want to contribute to the company's dominance in ... and my experience in ... will ensure I can" is a good strong answer. ("Not sure, really" or "It's close to the Dog and Duck bar" are not so good.)

What attracts you to this position?

Link your answer to your past experience. Thus: "When I was working at ... I realised how much I enjoyed ... and that I felt I could really develop a challenging career in ..." The key with this question is to demonstrate your ambition to develop your own career and abilities while at the same time contributing to the company's success.

Other perennial favourites include:

○ "Where do you see yourself in two years' time?"
○ "What's your greatest achievement?"
○ "Who or what has influenced you most?"
○ "What impression do you hope to give to strangers?"
○ "What is the capital of Peru?"(just kidding!)

Never admit to serious character weaknesses (everyone has them) but accentuate the positive at all times. Never be tempted to lie, blame others, or shrug your shoulders and say "I don't know".

❝ I find interviewing very difficult if there is little or no interesting information on the CV in front of me. It makes such a difference if there is something to hang a good question on. I always pick up on reasons why the candidate left a previous employer or anything out of the ordinary – Everest expeditions or a national prize win. It makes for a much easier flow of information. ❞
– Jimmy Green, healthcare manager

It is these types of questions you should find stock answers for before you go for your interview. If they trip off the tongue with confidence and sincerity you will impress the hardest nosed interviewer.

Building up to your interview

1. Don't try to reschedule an interview unless it is *absolutely* vital to do so. If there are genuine mega-reasons why you can't make it, be honest – phone up and explain.

2. Carefully read the letter offering you an interview. It will tell you the obvious things – place and time – but it should also make clear who will interview you and what you should bring. If it doesn't, phone and ask for full details.

3. If it will be expensive for you to attend, then find out if the company is prepared to pay. If it isn't, then it's your decision as to whether it will be worth it.

4. Think of the impression you will make. Your attire, hair, hygiene etc. should be designed such that there will be nothing about you to offend even the most closed-minded interviewer.

5. Practise being confident! Think about your handshake, posture and body language and the impression they will give to people who meet you for the first time.

6. Think about, and plan answers for, any obvious and/or awkward questions the interviewers are likely to ask you.

7. Research the company as much as is possible so that you at least know the basics of their business.

8. There is no such thing as the perfect candidate! Think about the positive things you can offer, and ways to divert attention from any possible weaknesses you may have.

What's in this chapter for you

Relaxed but prepared
Making an instant impression
When to listen ...
... and when to speak
Body language
Coping with the bad interviewer
Internal promotions

> 66 *It was a nightmare – late afternoon interview in the city and a call out of the blue from an old friend I'd not seen for years who'd just arrived back in town. Of course I met her for lunch! One wine turned into two bottles and, although I know I made it to the interview, I couldn't tell you how it went. There was nothing in the rejection letter to suggest that I'd behaved too badly, though.* 99
> **– Paula Springer, unemployed administrator**

We will not patronise you any more at this stage, as many other books do. We know you won't turn up for the interview drunk, stoned, hung-over, smelling of garlic or late!

Relaxed but prepared

Do ensure that you get to the venue with ten or fifteen minutes to spare in order to relax yourself and get your bearings. Be pleasant and friendly to the receptionist and to anyone else you meet – you never know how important they might be in the recruitment process!

It is worth a visit to the toilet, regardless of immediate need. You won't want to get caught short in the interview, but more important than that, you need the opportunity to finally tidy yourself up and cool yourself down (washing your hands in cold water will help avoid a sweaty handshake from you, if nothing else!).

If you can avoid doing so without getting in everyone's way and feeling awkward, resist the opportunity to sit down while you wait. If you are sitting down when summoned, you will be scrambling to your feet and starting the interview at a distinct disadvantage. Other tips while waiting are:

○ *Avoid conversation with other candidates if at all possible – their nerves may be contagious!*
○ *If you want to read, look at your notes or any company literature that is available.*
○ *Don't chew gum, smoke or fiddle with yourself!*
○ *Take deep breaths to control your nerves and keep telling yourself "I can do this!"*

You're on!

Finally, and it may seem to take an eternity to arrive, you are on! Someone will come and collect you from the waiting area and take you to the interview room. During the course of this journey, try some polite and pleasant small talk to establish that your mouth is still functioning.

When you enter the room, you will be introduced to the people interviewing you. You should already know the names of the key recruiter and should have tried to have found out everyone else's name and position beforehand, but if you are confronted by people you weren't expecting, try to listen out for their names. It will make a very good impression if you can reply to them in the interview by using their names correctly.

Other must do's when you first walk in are:

❑ *Smile and look everyone full in the face.*
❑ *Shake hands when it is expected (and remember, match their grip!)*
❑ *Sit down when you are asked to – remain standing if you are not.*
❑ *Remember your body language when sitting down.*
❑ *Put your case or bag behind you after you've taken out the things you need.*

❝ I try to put people at ease at the beginning of an interview by asking them if their journey was OK and if they had found us easily. I think it's important to try to relax the candidate as much as possible – it's meant to be an interview, not an interrogation! Intelligent candidates know this and keep their answers short, concentrating on getting the right volume and tone of voice. ❞
– Gill Jones, personnel manager

At this stage, the only thing you should have in your hand is a pen and some paper (preferably a diary or organiser) and you should be making brief notes when the job outline and company history is being given – however, concentrate on what is being said. Write down only key words relating to things that you had no knowledge of prior to the interview.

If you've followed our advice so far, you will already have predicted the obvious questions that you can expect. If the job is of a technical nature then you can expect some technical questions which your background research, experience and training should have prepared you for.

Experienced interviewers will ask you open questions (those beginning "how?", "when?", "why?", "where?" etc.) in order to encourage you to talk. Concentrate on giving full answers but avoid the temptation to waffle. You want to get over the pertinent facts about yourself, so know when to stop!

❝ I always throw in a closed question just to see what the response is! I ask something like "Did you enjoy your time at school?" and see if they are happy to respond with just "yes" or "no". Good candidates will answer in this way, but expand slightly. ❞
– Gill Jones

Deep water?

If you are younger and less confident there is always the danger that you may dry up or be unable to think of an answer. Don't worry, this happens to the best of people. Try asking for the question to be repeated if necessary (to give yourself some time to think) and if you can't then come up with a good answer, be honest and admit it. Don't be tempted to waffle on about something else – you'll only make things worse!

> Always try to turn lack of experience or knowledge to your advantage. For example, if the interviewer says, "You've no direct experience of...", then you can answer something like "No, but I think my great strength is flexibility and a willingness to develop new skills" and then go on if possible to cite an example from your past.

Other tips for interview success are:

○ *Don't interrupt your questioner – let them finish.*
○ *Don't repeat yourself.*
○ *Maintain good equal eye contact with each member of the interview panel when replying to a question. This does not mean staring them out, which can be viewed as being aggressive or threatening. Keep your eyes on each person's face without looking straight into their eyes.*
○ *Don't criticise past employees or teachers. Negativity and bad grace will get you absolutely nowhere.*

Be aware of the nice/nasty act. You may find that one person asks the easier, relaxing question whilst another goes for the jugular. Remember that you are not there to be intimidated so keep your cool and answer as best you can. If you consider a question to be deliberately obtuse and irrelevant, then ask for clarification before attempting an answer. If it is a genuine question badly put then you will understand it better; if it is just an attempt to rattle you, it will have failed.

Your questions

You will usually be given the opportunity to ask your own questions. You should have given this some thought before you got to the interview and written some themes down for possible questions. However, do not just trot these questions out for the sake of it – the chances are that quite a few issues will have been covered in the course of your discussion.

Ask questions when you are given the chance but make sure that they are relevant. Using the phrase, "I was particularly interested to learn about ..." will show that you have been listening and can think on your feet. If you have no outstanding questions, say so.

❝ The inexperienced applicants have obviously been told that, whatever happens, they've got to get in four or five of their own questions. Nothing is more off-putting than hearing pre-prepared questions trotted out regardless of the fact that they have been answered already. Don't these people listen to what is being said?! ❞

– Jane Lappet, accounts manager

Pick up on your interviewer's body language. They will be working to tight schedules themselves, so if they start appearing distracted, and keep looking at their watch, keep it brief. It doesn't necessarily mean that they are bored with what you have to say, just pushed for time.

If you really have to make another point even though the interview is running late, preface it with "I know that you are running to a tight schedule, but I have one last point to make..." Thus you show yourself to be caring and considerate, but also assertive.

Winding up

A professional interviewer should wind proceedings up, explain the next stage in the recruitment process and give a time scale in which you can expect to hear back from them. Should this not be made clear, you have every right to ask what happens next and when you can expect to hear.

Once the interview is declared to be over, thank everyone for their time and shake hands in a confident manner. As you reach the door, turn, smile, thank them again and leave, closing the door behind you.

Disaster scenarios

We've just looked at a fairly perfect interview scenario, when you've been listened to and allowed to speak, and when everything has run to time. However, many interviewers are not as professional as this, so what do you do if the interview goes badly?

> " *I was looking for work for about six months. In that period I was interviewed about eight times, each of them badly. They either didn't let me speak, didn't respond to what I had been saying or had obviously not scheduled themselves probably – they were more worried about the time than what it was that I was saying.* "
> **– Paula Reynolds, advertising executive**

Here are some handy tips to stop hopeless interviewers from wasting your time – and theirs!

Time-keeping

If they are obviously clock-watching and you've noticed a queue of other candidates outside, mention it! Be bold – say something like: "It is obvious that you are very pushed for time. Perhaps we can cut to the key issues which in my opinion are xyz, and then I could have a couple of minutes telling you why I think I am suitable for the job." It's bold and brash and it may get you thrown out. However, it is unlikely that anyone else will try it and it will get you respected and noticed!

Poor location

An interview should be conducted in a quiet, well-lit environment in which the furniture is not laid out as if by the local secret police for an interrogation. The interviewer should not allow him or herself to be interrupted except in the case of imminent Armageddon. If you find yourself being interviewed by someone with a dozen mobile phones and pagers, in a broom cupboard beside the machine tool room, you have three choices:

- ○ *Put up with it and shout*
- ○ *Ask if it is possible to relocate*
- ○ *Leave, assuming that a company who shows no respect for possible future employees is not going to be a great one to work for.*

Disorganised interviewer

Some interviewers are going to be as nervous as you are. This may manifest itself by way of shuffling of papers, scratching etc. etc. If you have the misfortune to be interviewed by a total incompetent, then you will probably just have to grin and bear it. The consolation is that you may be able to subtly hijack the interview and talk only about your excellent qualities. So long as you're polite and not too domineering, you could end up making a great impression.

Indiscreet/rude/racist/ageist interviewer

Quite simply, don't put up with any behaviour which you consider to be offensive. If an interviewer oversteps the mark, then tell them. If offensive behaviour is persistent, then leave politely. You should register your disapproval and then follow up with a full letter of complaint.

Turbo-verbosity

If you can't get a word in edgeways then you cannot really hope to make much of an impression. You can either sit there and try to nod at the right moments or, as politely as possible, interrupt – say things like, "I couldn't agree more" or "I'm pleased you said that as I feel…". A touch of sycophancy might just get you noticed!

If you are unfortunate enough to come across a poor interviewer, keep calm and be patient. Take any opportunity you can to get noticed and to try to get your points across politely and tactfully. Sympathise with their predicament but, at the same time, be determined to get your say.

Internal promotions

Very often a job will come up in an organisation that invites applicants from both inside and outside the organisation. If you find yourself in the situation of having to apply for a job within the company you are currently working for, you have certain natural advantages but there are also pitfalls that you need to be aware of.

> " *My boss told me that there was a new manager's job coming up and that they would like me to apply. He made it clear that I would need to compete against outsiders as the post was being advertised nationally. I knew that I had a good chance but wasn't complacent. I did all the preparation, worked really hard, then when I went into the interview and was faced by three people I knew well – my existing managers – I went to pieces. It was much worse than being interviewed by complete strangers.* "
> **– Judith Cooper, housing manager**

If you are going for an interview for a position in your current organisation, you should without doubt consider yourself to have certain advantages over outsiders. However, be aware of what Judith went through. It can be very disconcerting to be formally interviewed by people who you know well.

Here are some tips on how to approach the internal interview:

- ❑ *Try to forget any friendship you might have with the interviewers. At the interview keep it as formal and professional as possible and don't allow your guard to drop in any way. Remember, you are being judged against unknown competition.*
- ❑ *Don't compromise yourself by trying to find out "inside" information from anyone. This could damage your cause and make you appear to be trying to gain unfair advantage.*
- ❑ *Try to avoid excessive eye contact with any one person on the board.*
- ❑ *Use the knowledge that you have of the organisation constructively. Never criticise other departments. Suggest subtly how you would look to make improvements and introduce sensible change.*
- ❑ *Don't carp on about what is happening within the organisation. If they've advertised outside they may well be looking to introduce new ideas, not keep with what may be seen as the status quo. Try to find out as much as you can about what is happening in other organisations and then introduce this knowledge*

Although we can't promise you the job at this stage, we can promise that your self-esteem will be soaring after you pull off a great interview. This will fire you up for any other impending interviews you might have.

Tips for a successful interview

1. Tell yourself that you CAN get this job. Be determined to succeed and your confidence will shine through!

2. Get to the venue with enough time to get your bearings and to ensure you are relaxed. Tidy up in the toilet and wash your hands in cold water so your handshake isn't sweaty.

3. Remember and use the interviewers' names – it helps you to build a rapport and will make a very good impression in the first few minutes.

4. Concentrate on your body language as you sit down – lean towards the interviewer and smile enthusiastically. No shuffling and twitching! Maintain good eye contact at all times too.

5. You should have practised and rehearsed your answers to the obvious questions but don't be tempted to waffle if you are asked a technical question on your pet subject – keep it short and to the point.

6. Ask questions because you are genuinely interested in the answers, not for the sake of asking.

7. Pick up on your interviewer's body language and try to match it. You should watch for signs that suggest you are rambling – glazed eyes, head bowed – and be ready to check yourself.

8. If you feel a question is unfair or just plain rude, say so. Don't compromise yourself!

What's in this chapter for you

Doing a post mortem
The art of second interviews
Passing tests
Dealing with presentations
Dealing with failure

> 💬 *I came out of the interview with my head spinning. I was sure it had gone well, even though I'd been grilled on my lack of experience. Little did I know what was to follow.* 💬
> **– Piet Kotowski, systems planner**

Undoubtedly you will come out of the interview feeling somewhat exhausted, and either elated or despondent, depending on how you felt it all went. Relax – you deserve it – and try to forget about it all … at least for half an hour!

Once it is all over

You do need to try to remember the pertinent details of what was covered. For example, did they give a clear indication of the kind of salary that would be on offer? If so, write it down, so that it does not become lost in the mists of time.

Within an hour of coming out of the interview, go back over the events and make notes. Write down the facts as presented, then also think of the moments in the interview when you appeared to score points. What buttons did you press to get a good response? Where did you feel that you went wrong?

Some danger signs might be:

○ *Repeated questions on the same issue: you may have felt that you answered a particular question properly, but if they kept referring to the issue then there may well be something in your application that is giving them cause for concern. Try to work out what this may be – if you go back for a second interview, then you must be prepared to ease their worries.*

○ *Did the interviewer(s) appear unconvinced at any time? If so, why? Was it because of something in your experience, or something in the way you presented it? Either way, try to come up with ways to overcome such concerns next time.*

Don't spend hours on this deliberating. This stage of the recruitment process is over and there is nothing you can do about what is past. Make your notes, then relax! You will obviously be on edge to know if you have got the job, or if you are to be called for a second interview, but now try to forget about it and don't allow the experience to elate or deflate you.

Waiting to exhale

You should have been told at the interview when you will know if you have been successful. What should you do if the time has passed and you still have not heard?

> **"** *I was getting really desperate. It was the job I knew I wanted. They'd said that I'd hear in ten days but I'd heard nothing within two weeks. I thought, "what the hell" and got on the phone to them. It transpired that I was not the first choice but the other person was mucking them about over salary. As I was obviously keen, I got the job!* **"**
> **– Chris Wiley, salesman**

We believe that a company should behave with enough respect to you to honour any agreement they have made to let you know of your success or otherwise within a given time. If you haven't heard, then write or phone. Your determination might just tip the balance!

The second interview

Many companies will want to see candidates again, even for fairly junior positions. A second interview can, on the face of it, be seen to be as terrifying as the first and you might suffer feelings of "Oh God, not again!". Don't panic: in fact a second interview is a cause for celebration for the following reasons:

○ *You are already a success – getting this far is a major achievement*
○ *You know what to expect – you've been to the building, you've met the people and you have a feeling for the operation*

○ *You can identify your possible weak spots from the first interview and avoid them second time around*

The second interview is being held to reinforce the company's view of you – they may be looking to push you much further than last time so you can expect more detailed questioning on specific issues to do with your ability to do the job.

Some hot tips for approaching the second interview

❑ *Remember people's names and job titles so that you can address them properly the second time round without the need for more introductions.*
❑ *Refer to the notes you made after your first interview in order to anticipate problem areas and work out a response.*
❑ *Check your appearance again: try to avoid wearing precisely the same things as you did last time – you may not have two acceptable outfits but you can vary the one you have by changing your tie/scarf/shirt/blouse or whatever.*
❑ *Read and reread all of the information that you compiled for the first interview. You need to be absolutely confident that you know all there is to know about the company and that you cannot be caught out.*
❑ *Revise the questions that you asked last time.*
❑ *Beware interlopers! Find out who will be interviewing you second time around, and if the MD or CEO is to be involved, work on impressing him or her. They may be the ultimate decision makers.*

Before you attend the second interview, think about the job now you have had the chance to develop your ideas – imagine yourself in the position. What would you want to do in the first three months? The next three months? After the first year?

Many companies will use the second interview to really push you for serious ideas as to how you would approach the job. The research that you have done before the first interview will mean that you should have all of the facts about the business at your fingertips. Now, allocate some time to think strategically – imagine yourself in the job – what kind of things would you look at implementing?

Remember: the second interview, unlike the first one, is less about what kind of person you are and more about how you think and how you will cope in the job.

Tests

It may well be that at the second interview you will be asked to sit some kind of aptitude or intelligence test. This should be made very clear to you following the first interview or in the letter asking you to the second interview.

> Are the jobs you are aiming for likely to involve tests? If so, are you ready for them?

Psychometric tests have a slightly sinister image, but are used quite extensively in senior appointments. They are not used to test people's intelligence but rather to try to gauge what kind of person an applicant is. Hence you will tend to be asked questions which will reveal something of your attitudes and mindsets.

Such tests are normally used in conjunction with other factors and they have weaknesses. Some do not take properly into account racial or cultural differences, for example, so beware.

> Tests of any kind can be stressful and this, combined with an interview, could send the soberest of candidates rushing for a large brandy. Try to find out what sort of test it is before you get there by phoning for clarification.

You can only do so much practise for such tests. If they are going to ask you for information of a technical nature, read up if you need to on the most relevant information you can find.
Techniques for passing psychometric tests can be learnt. If you are unused to this kind of exam, then get some books (there are many available) and practice.

A contentious author statement now. Some people are hopeless at IQ tests. This in our view does not make them idiots or unemployable. If you struggle to identify the odd one out in a row of floral patterns, be bold – ask: does your inability to do so invalidate your other qualifications?

> ❝ *I remember as a fresh faced undergraduate I had to attend an interview which then involved an IQ test. I was hopeless at it and obviously failed miserably because the interviewer came up to me and told me that I had been really impressive up until the test. I looked him in the eye and asked him if he thought this invalidated my Classics degree in any way! He looked taken aback – I didn't get the job, but I felt good that I'd stood my ground!* ❞
> **– Peter Davies, publisher**

Test skills can be learnt. Practise as much as is possible if your job success is dependent upon it.

Presentations

If you are going for a more senior position, you may well also be required to make a short presentation to the interview board. We'd love to say that there is absolutely nothing to worry about but we would be lying – such a prospect can be terrifying and involves a lot of work.

The golden rules of presentation apply in the main to this situation. We have not got time in this book to do more than briefly outline these but there are some handy tips to get you off on the right track.

Giving a presentation

☐ *Prepare yourself! Even the most gifted of orators finds it hard to stand up and talk, even for a couple of minutes, off the tops of their head. Plan what you are going to say.*
☐ *Write down your presentation in full and learn the argument that you wish to put over. Don't be tempted to read verbatim what you wish to say, as that will sound stilted. Rather, from your full script, make notes in bullet point form which you can rely on to lead you step by step through your case.*
☐ *If you want to use slides or, more likely, an overhead projector, make sure you know how it works. If you can,*

practise beforehand, although most tend to work on roughly the same principles so practising anywhere will help.
- ❏ *Avoid trying to throw jokes in unless you are a natural comic. Keep it plain and to the point.*
- ❏ *Give hands-outs summarising your main points – this will greatly help to reinforce your message.*

If you know the people to whom you are having to present, try not to make too much eye contact with any one person. Pick a spot in the room and try to keep focused on that. If you are applying for an internal promotion, do not restrict your presentation to what is going on in the organisation now. Whenever possible, refer to other organisations and what their good and bad features are.

Most importantly, practise, practise, practise!

The job offer

In most cases a job offer will be made formally by letter with the terms and conditions laid out clearly. In some cases you may well receive a telephone call telling you of the decision and that a formal letter is in the post.

You will obviously need to write back to confirm your acceptance, if you are satisfied with the offer.

> ❝ *I had been interviewed by a large organisation and right the way through the process they kept on about the number and quality of the other applicants. I felt really privileged to have got that far. I was thrilled when I got a phone call from the director offering me the job. I accepted at once. When the letter arrived, you can imagine my anger when it turned out that they were offering 15% less than we had discussed. I wanted the job but I felt cheated.* ❞
> **– Steve Barker, travel consultant.**

Steve's situation is not untypical. Some firms will build themselves up and whet applicants' appetites, then try to save a few hundred pounds on salary.

> ❝ *I wanted the job, but I did not want to join a company and feel resentful from day one. They wouldn't move on increasing the salary immediately, but I pushed them to agree that they would give me the*

discussed salary after three months. I felt happier that
there had been a compromise and that they knew I was
not a pushover. **99**
— **Steve Barker**

Always try to establish the precise terms and conditions that are
on offer – the best time to do this is at the end of your interview
when you are given the opportunity to ask questions.

If you come across potential employers who have changed their
tune with regards to what is on offer, think very hard. Are they just
being mean, and, if so, do you want to work for a company like
that? Or do they have a case – are you a little underqualified and
in need of extra training? If you agree that it might be the latter,
then their reduced offer may well be valid.

Profit from failing

First of all, accept that few people succeed in all they do 100% of
the time. If you do get the proverbial smack in the teeth with a wet
fish every now and then, try not to let it get you down. Of course
you will be disappointed, but you must see these setbacks as part
of a learning curve.

In today's tough job market, some positions attract a couple
of hundred applications. Very often 90% of people are rejected
at the initial stage. That means 20 people get through to the
first interview. Three quarters of these will fail to reach the
second interview. Of the final five, one person is going to "get
lucky".

If you have recently suffered a setback and are feeling low,
analyse yourself. How can you improve your performance next
time? Where do YOU think it you could have done better? If
you were after a promotion with the company you are currently
with, then ask your boss or personnel officer, not "What did I do
wrong?" but "How could I have done better?"

❝ I was devastated when I failed to get the manager's job. I had been advised to apply for it and everyone I spoke to thought that I had a really good chance. However, after getting to the second interview stage, they appointed someone from outside. I was furious and very nearly walked out. The personnel director called me in and told me their reasons for the decision. Basically they wanted me to get a little more experience before promoting me. She also told me I interviewed really well! I felt much happier and sure enough, got a similar promotion six months later! ❞

– Keith Wareham, direct marketeer

Being successful in job hunting (as in life in general) is all about keeping a positive outlook. Don't think in terms of failure, rather in terms of continual learning experiences.

After the interview

1. Within the first few hours of your interview, do your own post mortem and make detailed notes.
2. Were there areas which seemed to concern the interviewers? If so, why? Work out a response to any such concerns so you can counter similar questioning in future.
3. If you have been told that will hear about the decision by a certain date but no word arrives, phone to find out why. Your enthusiasm may pay dividends.
4. If you get a second interview, ensure all of the details are clear: who will you be seeing, will you face tests? Phone for confirmation if not.
5. Second interviews are far more rigorous. You will be expected to show how you would perform. Using your notes from the first interview, imagine yourself doing the job and devise action plans which you could discuss with the interviewers.
6. If you will be tested in the second interview, or asked to give a presentation, get hold of books to give you some guidance and practise, practise, practise!
7. Some of us are simply not good at tests. If the test is plainly not job related, be bold and challenge its relevance versus your qualifications.

8. If you are offered the job but the conditions seem to have changed mysteriously by the time the appointment letter arrives, challenge them – unless you can see that you are obviously underqualified and will need more training than the company had bargained for.
9. Most importantly, don't take failure negatively. There will be dozens, if not hundreds, of applicants for every good job. The odds are never good so think of a rejection as a learning experience – where could you do even better next time?!

With careful preparation, some hard work and a positive attitude, employers will be begging you to take their jobs!